CLEVELAND

BROWNS TRIVIA

John F. Grabowski

Quinlan Press
Boston

To Trish and Elizabeth for their support and inspiration, and to three special little people in my life—Tommy, Sean and Melissa.

John F. Grabowski was educated in the City College of New York, where he was a member of the baseball team, and at Teacher's College, Columbia University, where he received his Masters in Educational Psychology. He currently teaches high school math and computer studies on Staten Island. When he is not teaching, he is a free-lance writer who has had several hundred pieces published in newspapers, magazines and the programs of professional sports teams. He is the author of *Super Sports Word Find Puzzles*, *Dodgers Trivia* and *San Francisco 49ers Trivia*, and was the publisher and editor of the monthly "Baseball Trivia Newsletter." He is also a nationally syndicated columnist, with his weekly *Stat Sheet* supplied to over six hundred newspapers by N.E.A.

I would like to thank Kevin Byrne and Francine Lubera of the Cleveland Browns, Jim Perry and the staff at NFL Properties, and Jim Scanlan of Quinlan Press.

Contents

The All-America Football Conference
Questions   1
Answers   7

NFL History
Questions   13
Answers   27

Offense
Questions   37
Answers   49

Defense
Questions   57
Answers   65

Coaches
Questions   71
Answers   77

Championship Games
Questions   83
Answers   97

Records and Honors
Questions   107
Answers   117

Miscellaneous
Questions   123
Answers   139

Photographs
Questions   149
Answers   177

The All-America Football Conference

1. Name the owner of the original Cleveland All-America Football Conference franchise.

2. Which National Football League club did he unsuccessfully attempt to buy before becoming owner of the Browns?

3. When a contest was held to come up with a nickname for the new team, what was the winning entry?

4. Why was the name eventually rejected?

5. Who was responsible for choosing the team's colors and uniform style?

The AAFC—Questions

6. Which division of the AAFC were the Browns members of?

7. What other clubs were in that division?

8. Where was the Browns' first training camp held?

9. Who was the first player signed by the Browns?

10. What was the result of the first exhibition game in Browns' history?

11. Who made Cleveland's first score in that game?

12. What was the Cleveland starting lineup for the first regular-season game in their history?

13. What was the result of that game?

14. Who combined on a 19-yard pass play for the Browns' first score in a regular-season game?

15. Who else scored for Cleveland?

16. What was the attendance for that first game?

17. Which five ex-Cleveland Rams signed with the Browns in 1946, rather than move to Los Angeles with the Rams?

18. What was the reason that Adams was allowed to remain with the Browns?

19. How many consecutive wins did they put together in 1946 before first tasting defeat?

20. Who finally beat them?

21. What was the name of the all-girl band formed by Mickey McBride that performed at halftime of Browns' games in 1946?

22. Which two black players did Cleveland sign in 1946 to break the color line in the AAFC?

23. In their maiden season, which team did Cleveland shut out twice?

24. Who was named to the AAFC All-Star squad in 1949 at center, even though he actually played linebacker?

25. Which other Browns were named to the squad?

26. Why didn't Y. A. Tittle play for the Browns after signing a contract with them in 1947?

27. When Lou Groza kicked his 11th field goal in 1946, he broke the pro record of 10 held by whom?

28. Who did the Browns obtain from Brooklyn in 1948 in exchange for the draft rights to Michigan All-America Bob Chappuis?

29. Cleveland rolled on to an undefeated season in 1948, despite losing this receiver for half a year with a broken leg. Name the receiver.

30. How did the Browns do financially that first season? Did they make or lose money?

31. In what year did Paul Brown go to an exclusive two-platoon system?

32. In 1947, which team did the Browns tie, 28-28, after trailing 28-0 at the half?

33. In 1948, what incredible feat did the Browns perform over the eight-day period from November 21 to November 28?

34. Which team tied Cleveland twice during the 1949 season?

35. Who was saluted at halftime ceremonies of the Cleveland-San Francisco game on October 27, 1946?

36. Who was the Browns' first opponent in their 29-game unbeaten streak?

37. Who finally ended the streak in October of 1949?

38. How did Cleveland do the following week?

39. What Cleveland records did Otto Graham and Dante Lavelli set in that game?

40. What unfortunate event also occurred in the game?

41. What was Cleveland's record during the streak?

42. With the Browns and Dons tied, 10-10, in a 1947 game, the Los Angeles kicker missed a field goal. The Browns, however, had 12 men on the field. Given another chance, the kicker connected, giving Los Angeles a 13-10 victory. Who was the placekicker?

43. Which Browns defender led the AAFC in interceptions their first season?

44. How many times did Otto Graham lead the AAFC in passing?

45. The Browns' 1949 exhibition against San Francisco was played as a benefit game. Who received the $25,000 that was raised?

46. Which AAFC clubs joined the National Football League with the Browns when the two leagues merged in 1950?

47. In the final game in AAFC history, the champion Browns were defeated by a league all-star team, 12-7. Name the future Browns quarterback who led the all-stars.

48. Name two future NFL stars who were drafted by the AAFC Browns and also by NFL teams, and were lost to Cleveland due to the terms of the merger.

49. Cleveland had the leading receivers in the AAFC in each of its four seasons. Can you name those players?

50. The Browns had only one AAFC rushing leader in those four years. In which season did Marion Motley finish first?

51. In which season did Cleveland score more points than in any other year in its history?

Answers

1. Taxicab company owner Arthur "Mickey" McBride

2. The Cleveland Rams

3. The Panthers

4. Coach Paul Brown did not want to be associated with a name which had been used by a failed NFL franchise. The Cleveland Panthers of the 1920's were such a club.

5. Coach Paul Brown

6. The Western Division

The AAFC—Answers

7.   The San Francisco 49ers, the Los Angeles Dons and the Chicago Rockets

8.   At Bowling Green University

9.   Otto Graham

10.   Cleveland 35, Brooklyn 20 (August 30, 1946)

11.   Running back Fred Evans, on a pass from Cliff Lewis

12.   Ends—Mac Speedie and Alton Coppage; tackles—Jim Daniell and Chet Adams; guards—Ed Ulinski and Bill Willis; center—Mo Scarry; quarterback—Cliff Lewis; halfbacks—Edgar Jones and Don Greenwood; fullback—Gene Fekete

13.   Cleveland shut out the Miami Seahawks, 44-0.

14.   Cliff Lewis and Mac Speedie

15.   Dante Lavelli, Tom Colella, Don Greenwood, Ray Terrell and Lou Groza

16.   Sixty thousand, one hundred and thirty-five, setting a then-professional football record

17.   Chet Adams, Gaylon Smith, Don Greenwood, Tom Colella and Mo Scarry

18. A court upheld the Browns' claim that Adams' contract was with the Cleveland, not Los Angeles, Rams.

19. Seven

20. The San Francisco 49ers, 34-20

21. The Musical Majorettes

22. Marion Motley and Bill Willis

23. The Miami Seahawks (44-0, and 34-0)

24. Lou Saban

25. End Mac Speedie and quarterback Otto Graham

26. He was assigned to the Baltimore Colts in a special dispersal draft designed to balance the league.

27. "Automatic" Jack Manders of the Chicago Bears (1934)

28. Dub Jones

29. Dante Lavelli

30. They made a profit of $200,000.

31. 1947

32.   The New York Yankees

33.   They won three games in three different cities (New York, Los Angeles and San Francisco).

34.   The Buffalo Bills (28-28, and 7-7)

35.   World War II hero General Jonathan Wainwright

36.   The Chicago Rockets, who lost 31-28, on October 19, 1947

37.   The San Francisco 49ers, winning by a score of 56-28, for Cleveland's worst AAFC defeat

38.   Following a dressing-down by Coach Brown, the Browns destroyed the Los Angeles Dons, 61-14.

39.   Graham passed for six touchdowns, Lavelli hauling in five.

40.   Halfback Edgar Jones suffered a broken collarbone, which ended his Cleveland career.

41.   Twenty-seven wins, no losses and two ties

42.   Ben Agajanian

43.   Tom Colella, with 10

44.   All four of its seasons

45.   The Cleveland Zoo

46.   The Baltimore Colts and the San Francisco 49ers

47.   George Ratterman

48.   Doak Walker and Lynn Chadnois

49.   Dante Lavelli (1946—tie) and Mac
Speedie (1947, 1948, 1949)

50.   In 1948 (964 yards)

51.   The team's first season, 1946 (423 points)

NFL History

1. What team did Cleveland play in its first NFL regular-season game?

2. How did the Browns do in their NFL debut?

3. Who kicked the five PATs for Cleveland in that game?

4. The NFL's leading rusher in 1949 sat out that game due to an injury. Who was he?

5. In the third game of the 1950 season the Browns were shut out for the first time in their history. Who blanked them?

6.   What was the final score?

7.   What else was noteworthy about the game?

8.   The Browns wound up tied with New York for the American Conference lead with a 10-2 mark. How did they do in the Playoff to decide the Conference champion?

9.   What was unusual about the Browns-Eagles game of December 3, 1950?

10.   Otto Graham completed one pass in the contest. Why was it erased?

11.   As a result of a merger deal with Buffalo, which three players did Cleveland obtain prior to the 1950 season?

12.   The only club to defeat Cleveland in 1950 was the Giants. What was the name of the defensive alignment the New Yorkers were known for?

13.   Who was the first team to defeat the Browns in an opening day game?

14.   What was the result of the Browns' first appearance against the Chicago College All-Stars?

15. Which two future Browns were in the All-Stars' starting lineup?

16. Which two rookie receivers helped lead the Browns to the 1952 Eastern Conference title?

17. In the 1952 Pro Bowl, Cleveland representatives accounted for all the American Conference points in their 30-13 loss. Who scored?

18. Which two players did the club lose to the Canadian Football League in 1953?

19. That same season, the Browns made a blockbuster 15-player deal with which club?

20. Who were the players that changed uniforms?

21. Who bought the team from McBride that year?

22. How much did they pay for the franchise?

23. Which three members of the original 1946 squad returned to the Browns following the 1953 season?

24. In 1954, the Browns had the number-one pick in the draft as a result of the bonus

pick, which they were awarded. Who did they choose?

25. Did he ever play for Cleveland?

26. Why was the 1954 Browns-Lions game at Cleveland Stadium rescheduled for December 19?

27. What was the greatest rout in Cleveland history?

28. With Lou Groza sitting out the second half of the game, who was called on to kick three PATs?

29. Which running back was billed as "the new Marion Motley" in 1954?

30. Which two Browns were called into the Air Force in 1955?

31. Which star retired following the 1955 season?

32. In 1955, which two players signed with both Cleveland of the NFL and Winnipeg of the CFL, prompting Winnipeg to sue the Browns?

33. What was the result of the 1955 Browns-Chicago College All-Stars game?

34. Which future Browns player started at left tackle for the All-Stars?

35. None of the Browns' first three picks in the 1955 draft ever played for Cleveland. Name them.

36. Who shared the quarterback chores in 1956—the Browns' first losing season?

37. What was their final record?

38. What unusual penalties were assessed against Cleveland in its December 2, 1956 game against the Philadelphia Eagles?

39. What was the result of the 1956 Browns-Chicago College All-Stars game?

40. Which future Browns player started at left halfback for the All-Stars?

41. Which year was the first in which the Browns were outscored by their opponents during the regular season?

42. What was noteworthy about the Cleveland-Detroit exhibition game in September of 1956?

43. When the Browns picked Jim Brown in the 1957 draft, how many players were chosen ahead of him?

44. Who were those players?

45. Who won the NFL's most valuable player award in 1957, when rookie Jim Brown finished tied for second with Colt quarterback Johnny Unitas?

46. What was the frightening finale of the Giants' 48-7 victory over Cleveland in New York, on December 6, 1959?

47. Which three Cleveland players were chosen by Dallas in the 1960 expansion draft?

48. What happened on the first play of the 1960 season, in the opening day game against Philadelphia?

49. Who purchased the Browns in 1961?

50. What was the selling price?

51. Who returned to the team in 1961 after a one-year retirement?

52. In 1961, who was Cleveland's opponent in the NFL's first Playoff Bowl for second-place finishers?

53. What was the final score of the game?

54. What was the Playoff Bowl also known as?

55. Name the New York Yankee catcher who was picked by the Browns in the ninth round of the 1961 draft.

56. Who was traded to Washington in 1962 in exchange for the number-one pick in the draft?

57. Who did Cleveland choose with the pick?

58. Did he ever play for Cleveland?

59. When did Cleveland host pro football's first doubleheader?

60. Who were the participants in this exhibition "Festival of Football"?

61. Which former sportswriter was named as Browns' general manager when Blanton Collier was appointed head coach in 1963?

62. Who did the Browns play in the second annual Hall-of-Fame game in Canton, Ohio, in 1963?

63. In which season did Cleveland first surpass 1 million in total attendance?

64. The Browns defeated the Giants, 52-20, on the last day of the 1964 season to clinch the divisional title. How well did

quarterback Frank Ryan pass that day statistically?

65. In which NFL season did the Browns score their most points ever?

66. How did Cleveland do in its fourth—and last—game against the Chicago College All-Stars in 1965?

67. Which future Browns head coach started on defense for the All-Stars?

68. Which future Brown started at defensive end for the All-Stars?

69. Who was the All-Stars' coach?

70. Which Cleveland star was seriously injured in the Browns' victory?

71. In a December 1966 game, the Browns and their opponents combined to score 89 points. Who did they play?

72. What was the final score?

73. In winning, the Browns had to come back from a deficit of how many points?

74. What season marked the first time in their history that the Browns lost their first two games?

75. What significant event occurred in 1967?

76. Who was Cleveland's first selection in the first combined NFL-AFL draft in 1967?

77. Which five Browns staged a joint strike of the Cleveland training camp in 1967?

78. How did the Browns do in their 1968 Playoff Bowl appearance?

79. How did Art Modell's actions solve the NFL-AFL merger problem and bring about peace between the two leagues?

80. Where was Modell at the time of the 1969 merger meeting?

81. Who did Cleveland defeat in 1970 in the first nationally televised Monday Night game? Where was the game played?

82. What was the attendance at that game?

83. Who was the first player to score in a Monday Night telecast?

84. Which player's 94-yard kickoff return for a touchdown was one of the highlights of the game?

85. What happened to the Browns in 1970 when the AFL merged with the NFL?

86.   How did they do in their first season in their new division?

87.   Who won the Central Division that season?

88.   What sad event occurred the week prior to Cleveland's 27-0 loss to Denver in 1971?

89.   The year 1972 marked the first time the Browns were winless in the exhibition season. What was their record?

90.   In 1972 Miami became the first NFL team to go through both the regular season and postseason without being defeated or tied. How did Cleveland do against them in the playoffs?

91.   Name the veteran guard who retired in 1973.

92.   What was unusual about the 1973 Pro Bowl?

93.   The Browns finished in last place for the first time in their history in 1974, with only their second-ever losing record. What was their mark?

94.   What was unusual about the first period of the Browns 15-10 loss to Buffalo in 1974?

95. What school did the team move its training quarters to prior to the 1975 season?

96. How many consecutive games did the Browns lose over the course of the 1974 and 1975 seasons?

97. What receiver returned to Cleveland in 1976 after a six-year absence?

98. Which player was lost to Tampa Bay in the 1976 expansion draft?

99. Which two players were lost to Seattle in the same draft?

100. Who were the Browns' opponents in the first overtime game in their history?

101. What was the result of the game?

102. What was unusual about the Browns' start in 1979?

103. Name the All-Pro guard who became available to Cleveland in a 1980 trade, following a contract squabble with Buffalo Bills head coach Chuck Knox.

104. What nickname was given to the 1980 Browns squad, due to their penchant for "heart-stopping" games?

105. Who intercepted Brian Sipe's final pass in the 1980 AFC Playoff, sealing the 14-12 win for eventual champion Oakland?

106. Why was the play controversial?

107. In what year did the Browns finish 5-11, yet still manage to defeat the two Super Bowl participants?

108. Who were the two teams, and what were the final scores of the games?

109. What dubious distinction did the Browns earn in the 1982 season?

110. What school became the new training home of the Browns in 1982?

111. What former NFL top draft pick did Cleveland sign that year, after he had played three seasons in the Canadian Football League?

112. Why did Art Modell threaten fines if Browns players shook hands with Rams players at midfield prior to their 1982 exhibition game?

113. What was the result when Cleveland played its first game after the strike was settled in 1982?

114. Which two Cleveland favorites did the club send to Oakland in separate deals on April 28, 1982?

115. 1985 marked the first time in NFL history that a team captured a division title with a non-winning record. What was Cleveland's mark that year?

116. Bernie Kosar set a postseason record for both pass attempts and yardage in the Browns' double-overtime victory over the Jets in 1986. What were his stats?

117. Whose roughing the passer penalty was a deciding play in the game?

118. Name the Denver Bronco whose 33-yard field goal in overtime ended the Browns' 1986 season.

119. The 1986 Browns won their double-overtime playoff game against the Jets, then lost the AFC Championship game in overtime to Denver, both by the same score. What was it?

Answers

1. The NFL champion Philadelphia Eagles

2. They defeated the Eagles by a score of 35-10. (September 16, 1950)

3. Chubby Griggs

4. Philadelphia's Steve Van Buren

5. The New York Giants

6. 6-0

7. It was Cleveland's first regular-season home game as a member of the NFL.

8. They beat the New Yorkers, 8-3.

9. The Browns were not credited with throwing a single forward pass in defeating Philadelphia, 13-7.

10. A pass to Dante Lavelli was called back because of a penalty.

11. Halfback Rex Bumgardner, guard Abe Gibron and tackle John Kissell

12. The "umbrella" defense

13. The San Francisco 49ers, 24-10, in 1951

14. They blanked the collegians, 33-0, in the 1951 contest.

15. Left tackle Bob Gain and right tackle Mike McCormack

16. Ray Renfro and Pete Brewster

17. Dub Jones, on a pass from Otto Graham, Lou Groza on two field goals, and Otto Graham on the extra point

18. Mac Speedie and John Kissell

19. The Baltimore Colts

20. Harry Agganis, Dick Batten, Gern Nagler, Bert Rechichar, Owen Scheetz, Ed

Sharkey, Don Shula, Art Spinney, Carl Taseff and Elmer Willhoite went to Baltimore in exchange for Tom Catlin, Don Colo, Herschell Forester, Mike McCormack and John Pettibon.

21. A group headed by Cleveland industrialist David Jones

22. Six hundred thousand dollars, the most ever for a pro football franchise at the time.

23. Bill Willis, Lin Houston and George Young

24. Quarterback Bob Garrett of Stanford

25. No. He was traded to Green Bay before the start of the season.

26. To avoid interference with the Indians-Giants World Series

27. Cleveland 62, Washington 3, on November 7, 1954

28. Defensive back Ken Konz

29. Maurice Bassett

30. Running backs Chet Hanulak and Billy Reynolds

31. Dub Jones

32. Quarterback Bobby Freeman and line-backer Jack Locklear

33. The All-Stars won, 30-27.

34. Jim Ray Smith

35. Center-linebacker Kurt Burris, halfback Dean Renfro and defensive tackle John Hall

36. Babe Parilli, George Ratterman and Tommy O'Connell

37. 5-7

38. A fifteen-yarder when fans pelted officials with snowballs following an unpopular call, and two five-yard penalties for excessive booing

39. Browns 26, All-Starts 0

40. Howard (Hopalong) Cassady

41. 1956 (177 to 167)

42. It marked the first game in which coach Paul Brown experimented with calling plays by way of a radio speaker placed in his quarterback's helmet. Cleveland lost, 31-14.

43. Five

44. Paul Hornung by Green Bay, Jon Arnett by Los Angeles, John Brodie by San Francisco, Ron Kramer by Green Bay and Len Dawson by Pittsburgh

45. Y. A. Tittle of San Francisco

46. Fans surged onto the field with two minutes to go. Many attacked coach Paul Brown, while others pulled down the goal posts. The game was held up for 20 minutes until order was restored.

47. Running backs Ed Modzelewski and Leroy Bolden, and wide receiver Frank Clarke

48. Eagle Timmy Brown took Lou Groza's kickoff five yards deep in the end zone and returned it 105 yards for a touchdown.

49. Former television and advertising executive Art Modell

50. $3,925,000

51. Kicker Lou Groza

52. The Detroit Lions

53. Detroit 17, Cleveland 16

54. The Bert Bell Benefit Bowl

55.   Quarterback Jake Gibbs

56.   Bobby Mitchell

57.   Heisman Trophy winner Ernie Davis of Syracuse

58.   No. He died of leukemia before appearing in an NFL game.

59.   On August 18, 1962

60.   Detroit played Dallas in the opener, with the Browns and Steelers meeting in the second game.

61.   Harold Sauerbrei

62.   The Pittsburgh Steelers

63.   1963 (1,086,879, including pre-season games)

64.   He completed 12 of 13 passes for 202 yards and five touchdowns.

65.   1964 (415)

66.   They won, 24-16

67.   Linebacker Marty Schottenheimer

68.   Jim Garcia

69. Former Brown Otto Graham, then coach of the Coast Guard Academy

70. Paul Warfield, whose broken collarbone kept him out of action for nearly the entire regular season

71. The New York Giants

72. Cleveland 49, New York 40

73. Twenty. They trailed at one point by a score of 34-14.

74. 1967

75. The NFL was realigned, and Cleveland was put into the Century Division.

76. Linebacker Bob Matheson of Duke

77. Leroy Kelly, Sid Williams, Mike Howell, John Brown and John Wooten

78. They lost to the Los Angeles Rams, 30-6.

79. He agreed to transfer the Browns to the American Football Conference, along with Pittsburgh and Baltimore.

80. In a New York hospital recovering from an ulcer attack

81. The New York Jets, 31-21, in Cleveland

82. 85,703

83. End Gary Collins, on an eight-yard pass from Bill Nelsen

84. Homer Jones'

85. The Browns became members of the AFC Central Division.

86. They finished second.

87. The Cincinnati Bengals, coached by former Cleveland coach Paul Brown.

88. Offensive backfield coach Sonny Keys died.

89. 0-6

90. They lost, 20-14

91. Gene Hickerson

92. It was the first one in which no Browns player participated.

93. 4-10

94. The Browns took the opening kickoff and held the ball for the entire first quarter.

95. Kent State University

96. Eleven

97. Paul Warfield

98. Wide receiver J. K. McKay, son of the Tampa Bay coach.

99. Defensive tackle Carl Barisich and guard-tackle John Demarie

100. The New England Patriots

101. Cleveland 30, New England 27

102. They won each of their first three games by three-point margins

103. Joe DeLamielleure

104. "The Kardiac Kids"

105. Safety Mike Davis

106. The Browns were on Oakland's nine yard-line with less than a minute to play. A field goal at that point would have won the game.

107. 1981

108. Cincinnati (20-17), and San Francisco (15-12)

109. They became the first team with a losing record (4-5) to make the AFC Playoffs.

110. Lakeland Community College

111. Tom Cousineau

112. Browns and Lions players had shaken hands prior to the first exhibition game as a show of solidarity, as the Players Association threatened a strike.

113. They defeated New England, 10-7.

114. Lyle Alzado and Greg Pruitt

115. 8-8

116. He completed 33 of 64 passes for 489 yards.

117. The Jets Mark Gastineau's

118. Rich Karlis

119. 23-20

Offense

1. How many times did Jim Brown gain 100 or more yards in a game in 1958?

2. What position did Brown play in college at Syracuse?

3. What Giants defensive player was his particular nemesis?

4. Which Cleveland back gained 232 yards rushing—on only 14 carries in a 1959 game against Washington?

5. In the same game, an opposing running back set a Washington record with 190 yards rushing of his own. Name him.

6. Who scored six touchdowns against the Bears in a 1951 game?

7. Who was Cleveland's opponent in a 1957 game when Jim Brown gained 237 yards rushing on 31 carries?

8. Who was the opponent when Brown gained 237 yards in a 1961 game, tying his record?

9. Name the quarterback who completed 11 consecutive passes in a 1960 game against the Redskins.

10. Who was nicknamed "Glue Fingers"?

11. Milt Plum had a string of how many consecutive passes thrown without an interception in 1959 and 1960?

12. Otto Graham threw six touchdown passes in a 1949 game against the Los Angeles Dons. What was the final score of the contest?

13. Which rookie running back led the Browns in rushing in 1956?

14. How many touchdowns did Lou Groza, the leading scorer in Browns history, score in his career?

15. Who was nicknamed "Grizzly"?

16. Who caught an 87-yard pass from Bill Nelsen in 1968 to set a Browns' NFL record?

17. What was Jim Brown's longest run from scrimmage?

18. Who did it come against?

19. Name the Browns' quarterback who once said, "I'm not a natural athlete. I pick up a dart and people start running"?

20. Which Browns end had a bone deficiency as a youngster which caused his left leg to be two inches shorter than his right?

21. Upon his retirement in 1970, this former Brown was the NFL's second all-time scorer, after Groza. Can you name him?

22. With Leroy Kelly out due to an injury, this running back had the best day of his career in Cleveland's 27-23 win over Washington in 1969. Who was this player who had a career-high 131 yards rushing?

23. What else was notable about that game against the Redskins?

24. How many touchdowns did Jim Brown score in 1965 to set a new NFL record?

25.   Which Cleveland back once rushed for exactly 1,000 yards in a season?

26.   This Browns player had only three receptions in 1980, but all three were good for touchdowns. Name him.

27.   Which Cleveland quarterback attempted, and completed, more than twice as many passes in his career as Otto Graham?

28.   What is wide receiver Rocky Belk's given name?

29.   Name the former Heisman Trophy winner who coached under Paul Brown at Great Lakes Naval Training Station in 1946, then played for him at Cleveland in 1949.

30.   Which NFL great, who lost the tip of his thumb in an accident as a youngster, finished his career as a member of the Browns in 1968?

31.   Which Browns quarterback twice completed 13 passes in succession while with Pittsburgh?

32.   Which Notre Dame coaching great played with the Browns in 1948 and 1949?

33. In how many consecutive seasons did Paul Warfield average more than 20 yards per catch?

34. What is the retired uniform number of Jim Brown?

35. What was his original number with Cleveland?

36. Which Cleveland running back ran for 202 yards against LSU in his first collegiate start his freshman year?

37. Who broke Lou Groza's club record for most field goals in a single season?

38. Name the running back who was the last player selected by Cleveland (10th, 280th overall) in the 1984 draft.

39. This Browns player is one of only two Colts to gain 1,000 yards rushing in a single season. Name him.

40. Jim Brown led the NFL in rushing eight times in his nine-year career. Which year did he fail to lead?

41. Who won the rushing title that season?

42. What was running back Pete Perini's given name?

43. How did the Browns do in Jim Brown's final NFL game?

44. Who took his place in the lineup the next season?

45. How much did Brown sign for as a rookie in 1957?

46. Which Cleveland receiver was the favorite target of Heisman Trophy winner Doug Flutie at Boston College?

47. Which Browns player once rushed for 347 yards in a college game against Wisconsin in 1968?

48. What happened to Bernie Kosar on his first play in pro ball?

49. How did he do passing after that?

50. What was the result of Kosar's first NFL start at quarterback?

51. How did Jim Brown do in his final pro game?

52. From which club did Cleveland obtain running back Ernie Green prior to the 1962 season?

53. How did Bobby Mitchell do in his first game back in Cleveland as a Washington Redskins?

54. How did Jim Brown and Johnny Unitas perform the first time they faced each other in the NFL?

55. In addition to football, what sport did Jim Brown star in at Syracuse?

56. What was Chick Jagade's given name?

57. Who is the youngest player to quarterback the Browns in their history?

58. Who broke Jim Brown's Cleveland rookie rushing mark?

59. Who is the NFL's all-time leading pass-catching tight end?

60. In 1985, this wide receiver broke Ray Renfro's Cleveland record for the best average per catch for a single season. Who is he?

61. Which Browns quarterback earned his Ph.D. in Mathematics while playing in the NFL?

62. Name the Browns' running back who at one time held the Detroit Lions' career rushing mark.

63. What was the nickname of former Browns end Frank Pitts?

64. How did Lou Groza do on "Lou Groza Day" in 1962?

65. Which Cleveland quarterback completed 13 passes in succession in a 1984 game against the Saints?

66. What is the retired uniform number of Otto Graham?

67. Name the Browns' center who collects Conan the Barbarian comic books.

68. Which Cleveland wide receiver was also drafted in baseball (by Cincinnati), and in basketball (by Kansas City)?

69. Who was nicknamed "Tonto"?

70. Which Browns running back rushed for the second-highest total of yards in his first two NFL seasons, second only to Jim Brown's 2,469?

71. Who was the first Browns player to combine for 2,000 net yards in a season?

72. Which quarterback completed 11 consecutive passes against Pittsburgh in a 1956 game?

73. Name the star receiver who was released by both the Cowboys and Giants, signed

with the Patriots, then came to the Browns in a trade.

74. Which third-string quarterback started the Detroit game in 1975 due to the ineffectiveness of Brian Sipe and Mike Phipps the week before?

75. What was the result of Jim Brown's first NFL pass?

76. What was Edgar Jones' nickname?

77. Who was the back who averaged more than 17 yards per carry in a 1950 game against Pittsburgh?

78. 1971 saw the Browns employ only the third regular left tackle in the club's 25-year history. Who was the man who followed Lou Groza and Dick Schafrath?

79. What remarkable feat did Bobby Mitchell perform in Cleveland's 28-14 victory over Philadelphia in 1958?

80. Which Browns player made an 18-yard gain on his only rushing attempt of the 1985 season?

81. Who was nicknamed "Skeets"?

82. Name the Green Bay player who returned

two kickoffs for touchdowns against Cleveland in a 1967 game.

83. What was Lou Groza's highest single-season point total? In what season were they scored?

84. Where was Jim Brown born?

85. In which year did two Browns both reach the 100-point mark in scoring?

86. Who were they?

87. Who were Paul Brown's "messenger guards" in 1962?

88. Who finished second to Jim Brown in rushing on the 1962 squad?

89. Who is the only Browns quarterback since 1950 to have more than one pass completion of greater than 80 yards to his credit?

90. The Browns twice have scored 62 points in an NFL regular-season game. Who were their opponents?

91. Which 23rd-round draft pick made the 1950 club as a running back?

92. Who had a 61-yard run from scrimmage on the first play of the game for the

Browns against San Diego on September 29, 1985?

93. What position did Otto Graham play in college?

94. Who was nicknamed "Jubilee"?

95. This running back's touchdown against Cleveland in 1985 moved him into second place on the all-time NFL list, behind Jim Brown. Who is he?

96. Which future Browns player scored the opening touchdown for the Chicago College All-Stars in their 27-7 victory over the Redskins in 1943?

97. Name the guard who played 16 seasons with the Browns.

98. Despite having already signed with Winnipeg of the CFL, this quarterback decided to play for Cleveland when the Browns drafted him in the third round in 1955. Can you name him?

99. Which tackle played for Cleveland from 1950 to 1952, jumped to the CFL, then returned to the Browns in 1954?

100. How did Heisman Trophy winner Charles White do in his professional debut?

101. Name the Browns' running back who made an 87-yard touchdown run in a 1950 exhibition game, but later did not remember scoring, because he suffered a slight concussion.

102. Lou Groza scored his 1,000th career point against which club?

103. Name the quarterback who was a back-up to All-America Johnny Lujack at Notre Dame.

104. Who is nicknamed "The Ice Cube"?

105. Which former Browns player is the AFL's all-time leader in touchdown passes thrown?

Answers

1. Nine

2. Halfback

3. Linebacker Sam Huff

4. Bobby Mitchell

5. Johnny Olszewski

6. Dub Jones

7. The Los Angeles Rams (November 24, 1957)

8. The Philadelphia Eagles (November 19, 1961)

9. Milt Plum

10. Wide receiver Dante Lavelli

11. Two hundred and eight

12. Cleveland 61, Los Angeles 14

13. Preston Carpenter

14. One

15. Tackle Bob Lingenfelter

16. Milt Morin

17. Eighty yards

18. The Washington Redskins (September 15, 1963)

19. Frank Ryan

20. Mac Speedie

21. Sam Baker

22. Reece Morrison

23. It was Cleveland's only regular-season victory over a team coached by Vince Lombardi.

24.   Twenty-one

25.   Greg Pruitt (1976)

26.   Keith Wright

27.   Brian Sipe

28.   Anthony

29.   Les Horvath

30.   Tommy McDonald

31.   Bill Nelsen

32.   Ara Parseghian

33.   Seven

34.   32

35.   45. He was given number 32 when running back John Bayuk was released during preseason.

36.   Greg Allen

37.   Matt Bahr (24 in 1984)

38.   Earnest Byner

39.   Curtis Dickey

40.   1962

41.   Jim Taylor of the Green Bay Packers

42.   Evo

43.   They lost the NFL championship game to Green Bay, 23-12. Brown gained only 50 yards rushing in 12 carries.

44.   Leroy Kelly

45. $15,000

46.   Brian Brennan

47.   Ron Johnson

48.   He fumbled his first snap from center.

49.   He completed his first 7 passes, winding up with 9 completions in 15 attempts, and 1 interception.

50.   He led Cleveland to a 21-6 victory over Houston (October 13, 1985)

51.   He scored three touchdowns for the East in its 36-7 win over the West in the 1966 Pro Bowl.

52.   The Green Bay Packers

52

53. He caught a Norm Snead pass for the winning touchdown as Washington won, 17-16.

54. Brown led Cleveland to a 38-31 victory, with 178 yards rushing, and five touchdowns. Unitas passed for four touchdowns.

55. Lacrosse

56. Harry

57. Bernie Kosar (21 years, 10 months, 11 days)

58. Kevin Mack (1,104 yards in 1985)

59. Ozzie Newsome

60. Clarence Weathers

61. Frank Ryan

62. Nick Pietrosante

63. "Riddler"

64. He kicked two field goals as the Browns defeated Dallas, 19-10, on October 7 1962

65. Paul McDonald

66. 14

67. Mike Baab

68. Dave Logan

69. Johnny Brewer

70. Earnest Byner (1,428)

71. Jim Brown (2,131 in 1963)

72. George Ratterman

73. Reggie Rucker

74. Will Cureton

75. A 37-yard touchdown to Ray Renfro on November 12, 1961, in a 17-6 victory over Washington

76. "Special Delivery"

77. Marion Motley (11 carries for 188 yards)

78. Doug Dieken

79. He returned a kickoff 98 yards for a touchdown and a punt 69 yards for a touchdown-both in the first quarter of the game!

80. Wide receiver Clarence Weathers

81.   Running back Volney Quinlan

82.   Travis Williams

83.   115 in 1964

84.   St. Simons, Georgia

85.   1968

86.   Leroy Kelly (120), and Don Cockroft (100)

87.   Gene Hickerson and John Wooten

88.   Quarterback Frank Ryan

89.   Bill Nelsen—87 yards to Milt Morin (November 24, 1968) and 82 yards to Paul Warfield (December 14, 1969)

90.   The New York Giants (December 6, 1953) and the Washington Redskins (November 11, 1954)

91.   Dom Mosselle

92.   Kevin Mack

93.   He was a single-wing tailback at Northwestern

94.   Wide receiver Allen Dunbar

95.　John Riggins

96.　Bob Steuber

97.　Gene Hickerson

98.　Bobby Freeman

99.　John Kissell

100.　He rushed for eight yards in three carries in the Browns' 48-0 loss to Kansas City.

101.　Don Phelps

102.　The St. Louis Cardinals (September 20, 1964)

103.　George Ratterman

104.　Gerald McNeil

105.　Len Dawson (182)

Defense

1. Who was nicknamed "Golden Domer"?

2. Which Browns defensive end was a third-round selection of the Phoenix Suns in the 1981 National Basketball Association draft?

3. Don Fleming's uniform is one of five retired by Cleveland. What was his number?

4. Who was the rookie who led the 1975 squad in sacks with eight?

5. Who is the only Cleveland player since

1950 to lead the Browns in interceptions *and* average over 30 yards per return?

6. Which Browns player was an All-America linebacker as well as an All-America heavyweight wrestler at Notre Dame?

7. Name the Browns' linebacker who has both a brother and father who played in the NFL.

8. What is the nickname given to the Browns' defensive unit?

9. Who is credited with giving them this appellation?

10. Name the Browns' linebacker who had a part in the movie *Paper Lion,* based on George Plimpton's book.

11. What was defensive tackle Chubby Griggs' given name?

12. Which former Browns player was the president of the New York Yankees from 1981 to 1983?

13. Who was the only Cleveland player selected for the Pro Bowl in 1979?

14. Which Yankton College graduate became Cleveland's inspirational force on defense

when the Browns won the AFC Central Division title in 1980?

15. Name the linebacker who returned to the Browns in 1954 after being out of football the previous two seasons.

16. Who led Cleveland in quarterback sacks each of the first four seasons in which records were kept?

17. Which Browns player once returned a fumble 89 yards for a touchdown?

18. What defensive end received a D.D. degree from Southwest Baptist Theological Seminary and went on to become an evangelist?

19. Who was nicknamed "Hum"?

20. Who was the former Browns linebacker who replaced the great Joe Schmidt in the middle for the Lions in 1966?

21. Which former Browns player was a member of the Minnesota Vikings' "Purple People Eaters" defense?

22. This former Browns player had appeared in 180 consecutive games at the time of his retirement in 1966. Can you name him?

23. Who was the defensive tackle who was waived to Atlanta in 1969 after being mistakenly placed on waivers after walking out of training camp?

24. Which defensive stalwart suffered a near-fatal staph infection late in 1979?

25. The player signed to replace him was driving a truck at the time. Who was he?

26. With which team did Len Ford end his NFL career?

27. Name the Browns' defensive back who wrote a book criticizing pro football?

28. What was the title of the book?

29. Who led Cleveland with 14 quarterback sacks in 1984?

30. Name the AFC Defensive Rookie of the Year from the Browns for 1984, as picked in a vote of his fellow players.

31. Which Brown linebacker shaves his head each training camp?

32. Who was Cleveland's only Pro Bowl selection in both 1983 and 1984?

33. What is former Browns linebacker Chip Banks' given name?

34. Who did legendary coach Woody Hayes call, ". . . the best-conditioned athlete I've ever coached"? He later played for the Browns.

35. Which Browns player made his first professional touchdown on a 55-yard blocked field goal against Green Bay in 1972?

36. Which defensive back was the 24th-round draft pick of Cleveland in 1952?

37. What is Junior Wren's given name?

38. Several Browns have intercepted three passes in a single game since 1950. Who is the only player to accomplish the feat more than once?

39. Cleveland's all-time leader in pass interceptions was their top draft pick in 1972. Name him.

40. Which player, who was a car salesman at the time, was signed by the Browns to replace Chuck Noll in 1957? Noll had suffered a broken arm in a game against the Cardinals.

41. In the Browns' 37-21 win over Detroit in 1964, who intercepted a pass on the last play of the game and returned it 65 yards for a touchdown?

42. Name the linebacker who was obtained in a trade with Green Bay, refused to report to Cleveland, changed his mind, vetoed a trade to the Rams, then was sent to the Lions? All this took place within a span of less than five months in 1957.

43. Which former Brown once fought Muhammad Ali in an exhibition match?

44. Who was nicknamed "Tombstone"?

45. What football team did Tom Cousineau play for upon leaving Ohio State?

46. Who returned an interception 88 yards for a touchdown against Dallas in Cleveland's 1969 Playoff win?

47. Who picked off passes in seven straight games for the 1968 squad?

48. Name the player who recovered five opponents' fumbles in 1954 for a Cleveland NFL mark.

49. Who is Cleveland's all-time leader in sacks?

50. In speaking of a teammate, one Browns player said "he . . . lived in outer space and spent most of his time on Mars." To whom was he referring?

51.   Who was nicknamed "Bam Bam"?

52.   Who was the first Browns' player to be named as a linebacker on an NFL All-Pro team?

53.   Which player was included in the 1985 trade with Buffalo for the draft rights to Bernie Kosar, but refused to report?

54.   Which Cleveland defensive tackle won the Outland Trophy in 1950?

55.   What was Jerry Sherk's nickname?

56.   Although he made his name with Chicago, this 6-foot, 8-inch defensive end was Cleveland's number-one draft pick in 1953. Can you name him?

57.   Who returned two interceptions for touchdowns in a 1960 game against Chicago to become only the third player in history to do so?

58.   Who was known as "Wild Man"?

Answers

1. Defensive back Tom Schoen

2. Sam Clancy

3. 46

4. Defensive back Mack Mitchell

5. Ken Konz (1958)

6. Bob Golic

7. Clay Matthews (father Clay, brother Bruce
   of the Houston Oilers)

Defense—Answers

8.   "Dogs"

9.   Cornerback Hanford Dixon

10. Mike Lucci

11. Forrest

12. Lou Saban

13. Defensive back Thom Darden

14. Defensive end Lyle Alzado

15. Tony Adamle

16. Defensive end Bill Glass (1964-67)

17. Defensive back Don Paul (November 10, 1957, versus Pittsburgh)

18. Bill Glass

19. Linebacker Weldon Humble

20. Mike Lucci

21. Defensive end Jim Marshall

22. Defensive tackle Dick Modzelewski

23. Bill Sabatino

24. Defensive tackle Jerry Sherk

25. Henry Bradley

26. The Green Bay Packers (1958)

27. Bernie Parrish

28. *They Call It A Game*

29. Defensive end Reggie Camp

30. Safety Don Rogers

31. Eddie Johnson

32. Linebacker Chip Banks

33. William

34. Tom Cousineau

35. Cornerback Clarence Scott

36. Junior Wren

37. Lowe

38. Tommy James (November 15, 1950, and November 1, 1953)

39. Thom Darden

Defense—Answers

40. Stan Sheriff

41. Defensive back Walter Beach

42. Roger Zatkoff

43. Lyle Alzado

44. Defensive end Richard Jackson

45. The Montreal Alouettes of the Canadian Football League

46. Defensive back Walt Sumner

47. Defensive back Ben Davis

48. Len Ford

49. Jerry Sherk (69)

50. Chip Banks

51. Linebacker Dick Ambrose

52. Tony Adamle (1951)

53. Chip Banks

54. Bob Gain

55. "The Sheik"

Defense—Answers

56.   Doug Atkins

57.   Bobby Franklin

58.   Defensive end Bob Oliver

Coaches

1. Who were the Browns' five assistant coaches in their maiden season of 1946?

2. Who is the only person to coach a championship club in both the AAFC and NFL?

3. Where did Paul Brown attend college?

4. Name the college where Paul Brown was head coach from 1941 to 1943.

5. What team did Cleveland beat in 1955 for Paul Brown's 100th career pro victory?

6. What team was the victim of Paul Brown's 100th NFL victory?

7. What team was the victim of Paul Brown's final win as coach of Cleveland?

8. Who took over as head coach when Forrest Gregg was fired at the end of the 1977 season?

9. In what capacity did former head coach Blanton Collier return to the Browns in 1975?

10. What move by owner Art Modell gave coach Sam Rutigliano even more power in 1981?

11. Which Cleveland head coach played in 188 consecutive NFL games?

12. Name the assistant coach who was also an assistant with the Kansas City Chiefs for 15 years before coming to Cleveland.

13. Which other NFL team did Paul Brown coach after leaving Cleveland?

14. Who was the first Browns' head coach to compile a lifetime losing record with Cleveland?

15. Which former assistant coach is the only man ever to win championships in both the NFL and AFL?

16.   Who did Marty Schottenheimer play for in the pros?

17.   What position did he play?

18.   How did the Browns fare in Nick Skorich's regular-season debut as head coach in 1971?

19.   How did Cleveland do in his first full year at the helm?

20.   Which two men were each assistant coaches with Cleveland for over 20 years?

21.   Who succeeded Blanton Collier as head coach in 1971?

22.   Which former USFL head coach was hired as the Browns' offensive coordinator in 1986?

23.   Can you name the former Browns' assistant coach who organized the NFL Players Association in 1956?

24.   Which Cleveland head coach used to warn his players at training camp, "If you cheat, your wives will be the first to know because I'll tell them"?

25.   Which current assistant coach was a former head coach of the Pittsburgh Maulers of the USFL?

26. What year did Marty Schottenheimer replace Sam Rutigliano as head coach?

27. Which Browns assistant coach was hired by Baltimore as their head coach in 1954?

28. Marty Schottenheimer was an assistant coach with what other teams in the NFL?

29. This former Browns assistant coach had interceptions in six consecutive games for Cleveland in 1960. Can you name him?

30. Which assistant coach jumped from the Cleveland Rams to the Browns in 1946 in order to stay in Cleveland rather than move to Los Angeles with the Rams?

31. Can you name the four assistant coaches who left Cleveland following the 1982 season?

32. How many times in his years at Cleveland did Paul Brown's club finish with a record under .500?

33. Nick Skorich's final game at the helm of the Browns was also the final game for his opposing number. Can you name this Houston Oilers coach who moved up to the front office?

34. Who took over as Cleveland's head coach in 1963 when Brown was fired?

35. What was Paul Brown's overall record as Cleveland coach?

36. Who was named head coach in 1975?

37. Which former Heisman Trophy winner was an assistant coach with the Browns in 1972 and 1973?

38. What happened to Paul Brown after his firing in 1963?

39. Which former Cleveland coach was head coach of the Eagles from 1961 to 1963?

40. Who was the assistant coach who was a college basketball teammate of NBA great Willis Reed at Grambling?

41. Which coach earned a reputation for holding a jinx over Paul Brown?

42. What pro team did Nick Skorich play for?

43. What position did Skorich play?

44. How many years did Paul Brown coach Cleveland?

45. Following Forrest Gregg's dismissal, who served as head coach for the final game of the 1977 season?

46. When Blanton Collier left Cleveland as assistant coach, he took over the head coaching job at the University of Kentucky. Who did he replace?

47. Who was hired in 1982 as the first strength coach in Browns' history?

48. Aside from Paul Brown, who is the only head coach who was not previously an assistant coach with the Browns?

49. Which ex-assistant coach was the former holder of the NFL record for receptions in a career?

50. Which former Browns player joined the club as tackle coach, replacing Weeb Ewbank, in 1954?

51. What is Weeb Ewbank's given name?

52. Where was Paul Brown coaching when he was hired by Cleveland in 1945?

53. Which former assistant coach was the first player to wear glasses in an NFL game?

Answers

1. John Brickels, Blanton Collier, Red Conkright, Fritz Heisler and Bob Voigts

2. Paul Brown

3. He enrolled at Ohio State, but transferred
   to and graduated from Miami (Ohio). He
   received his master's degree from Ohio
   State.

4. Ohio State

5. The Green Bay Packers (41-10, on October 23, 1955)

6. The Pittsburgh Steelers (30-28, on October 22, 1961)

7. The San Francisco 49ers (13-10, on December 15, 1962)

8. Sam Rutigliano

9. He returned as quarterback coach.

10. Modell named Rutigliano as a vice president of the team.

11. Forrest Gregg

12. Tom Pratt

13. The Cincinnati Bengals

14. Forrest Gregg (18-23-0, .439)

15. Weeb Ewbank

16. The Buffalo Bills (1965-1968) and the Boston Patriots (1969-1970)

17. Linebacker

18. They shut out Houston, 31-0

19. They won their first AFC divisional title, finishing 9-5, but lost to Baltimore in the playoffs.

20. Fritz Heisler (25 years, from 1946 to 1970), and Howard Brinker (22 years, from 1952 to 1973)

21. Nick Skorich

22. Lindy Infante

23. Creighton Miller

24. Paul Brown

25. Joe Pendry

26. 1984

27. Weeb Ewbank

28. The New York Giants and the Detroit Lions

29. Jim Shofner

30. Red Conkright

31. Rich Kotite, Rod Humenuik, Paul Hackett and Len Fontes

32. Only once, in 1956

33. Sid Gillman

34. Blanton Collier

35. 158-48-8, with 111-44-5 record in the NFL

36. Former Packer star Forrest Gregg.

37. John David Crow

38. He was retained by Cleveland as a vice president, and also remained as a stockholder.

39. Nick Skorich

40. Buck Buchanan

41. Buddy Parker of Detroit

42. The Pittsburgh Steelers (1946-1948)

43. Guard

44. Seventeen years, from 1946 to 1962

45. Dick Modzelewski

46. Bear Bryant

47. Former Nebraska defensive end Dave Redding

48. Sam Rutigliano

49. Raymond Berry

50. Ed Ulinski

Coaches—Answers

51. Wilbur

52. At the Great Lakes Naval Training Station

53. Raymond Berry

Championship Games

1. What was the result of the Browns' first AAFC Championship game?

2. What was their record against the New Yorkers in the regular season?

3. Which player made the first score in AAFC Championship game history?

4. Who scored first for Cleveland?

5. Whose catch of an Otto Graham pass gave the Browns their second, and final, score of the game?

6.   Who was the leading rusher in the contest?

7.   Name the coach of the New York club.

8.   The AAFC's regular-season rushing leader played for the Yankees. Can you name him?

9.   Where was the Championship game held?

10.   What were the field conditions that day?

11.   What was unusual about the PAT following Saunders' touchdown?

12.   Who intercepted an Ace Parker pass and sealed the game for the Browns?

13.   Beginning that maiden season of 1946, how many consecutive championship games did the Browns play in?

— 1947 —

14.   What was the outcome of the final 1947 game?

15.   For the second consecutive year, Cleveland's first score came on a one-yard run. Who scored the touchdown?

16. Who made the PAT following Cleveland's second score of the game?

17. Name the Browns' player who punted five times, good for a 45-yard average.

18. Who fumbled twice for the New Yorkers?

— 1948 —

19. What was the result of the 1948 contest?

20. Which eight Browns won spots on either the first or second all-league teams?

21. Before meeting Cleveland for the championship, which team did Buffalo have to defeat in a divisional playoff?

22. Whose interception led to Cleveland's first score of the game?

23. Which future Browns' player was the quarterback who led the Buffalo offense?

24. A Rex Bumgardner fumble was converted into Cleveland's second score. Who scored the touchdown on an 18-yard return of the fumble?

25. The Bills made their only touchdown on a pass to Al Baldwin from the quarterback who replaced Ratterman. Name him.

26. How many interceptions did Cleveland make that afternoon?

27. Buffalo gained only 63 yards rushing in the game. Marion Motley gained more than twice that amount by himself. How many yards did he gain?

— **1949** —

28. What was the score of the final AAFC Championship Game?

29. In what way were these playoffs different from the three previous ones?

30. What were the results of these games?

31. The San Francisco coach was the only man besides Paul Brown to coach his club in all four AAFC seasons. Who was he?

32. How many yards did league-leader Joe Perry gain in the contest?

33. When was the NFL-AAFC merger announced?

— **1950** —

34. Specifically, how did the Browns win their first NFL Championship Game?

35.   What happened on the first play from scrimmage?

36.   Trailing 28-20, the Browns came back to within a point on a diving touchdown catch by what receiver?

37.   How much time remained when Groza kicked his 16-yard field goal to win the game?

38.   How many yards did the NFL's leading rusher, Marion Motley, gain in the game?

39.   Who was the head coach of the Browns' first NFL championship opponent?

40.   Both clubs were forced into playoffs before advancing to the championship game. What were the results of those contests?

41.   Whose interception sealed the victory with less than half a minute to go?

42.   Following the game, what comment did NFL Commissioner Bert Bell make about the Browns?

— 1951 —

43.   1951 marked the first time in their history that Cleveland lost a championship game. Who defeated them?

87

44. How did the Browns' first drive of the game, perhaps an omen of things to come, end?

45. Lou Groza hit a field goal in the second period to put Cleveland on the scoreboard. How long was his playoff-record kick?

46. Despite their slow start, the Browns led 10-7 at halftime. Whose touchdown gave Los Angeles the lead for good in the third period?

47. Who led all rushers in the game with 43 yards?

48. With Norm Van Brocklin relieving Bob Waterfield, the Rams scored the deciding points on a 73-yard pass to whom?

49. Which two Browns collided while trying to cover him on the play?

50. The 1951 championship game was the first to be televised coast-to-coast. Which network carried it?

51. How much did it pay for the rights to it?

— 1952 —

52. In 1952, Cleveland once again lost the championship game. Who defeated them?

53. Who did Detroit beat in the division playoffs to gain the right to face the Browns?

54. Which three Cleveland players missed the game due to injuries?

55. Whose 67-yard touchdown run increased the Lions' lead to 14-0 in the third quarter?

56. How many touchdowns had he scored that season?

57. Who accounted for the Browns' only score of the game?

58. How many total yards and first downs did the Browns amass in the game?

59. Ahead 14-7, Detroit was forced to punt late in the game. Who fumbled the kick, giving the Lions possession of the ball, and the chance to put the icing on the cake with Pat Harder's 36-yard field goal?

60. A last gasp by the Browns was a Graham pass into the end zone, which was declared an illegal catch. What was the reason?

61. Who was the charismatic leader of the Lions?

— 1953 —

62. What was the result of the 1953 game?

63. The game marked Otto Graham's worst performance as a pro. What were his stats?

64. Who scored Cleveland's only touchdown, and also gained 104 yards rushing in the game?

65. What was unusual about Jagade's performance?

66. Who scored the game-winning touchdown on a 33-yard pass from Layne with just two minutes to play?

67. The above-mentioned player was in the lineup due to an injury to which Lion starter?

68. Whose interception of a last-minute Graham pass finished off the Browns?

— 1954 —

69. Who did the Browns trounce, 56-10, in the 1954 game?

70. Why was the game especially significant for Cleveland?

71. Did Graham play the following season?

72. How did Graham do statistically in the contest?

73. Despite the final score, the Browns' opponent outgained Cleveland in total yardage, 331 to 303. Who was the leading rusher for the Browns?

74. How many turnovers did the other team commit?

75. Who was the starting center for the Browns when they won the title in 1954, and the starting center for the Lions when they beat Cleveland for the title three years later?

— 1955 —

76. How did Cleveland do in the 1955 championship game, after which Graham retired for good?

77. Who was the rookie coach of the Rams?

78. A 65-yard interception return of a Norm Van Brocklin pass gave Cleveland a 10-0 lead in the second period. Who picked off the toss?

79. How did Graham do statistically in his second farewell?

91

80. Who led the Browns in rushing with 61 yards?

81. The game was played before a record crowd for a championship game. How many fans were in attendance?

82. With what remarkable record did Graham end his career?

83. How many Rams passes were intercepted by the Browns?

84. What was the result of Graham's final NFL pass?

— 1957 —

85. How did the Browns do in the championship game in 1957?

86. Who did Detroit beat in the divisional playoff in order to advance to the championship contest?

87. Which reserve fullback was the star of the game for the Lions?

88. Why was Tobin Rote at quarterback for Detroit?

89. Who was the Lions' coach?

90. How did he come to be head coach?

91. A faked field goal attempt was a key play early in the game. Who took holder Rote's pass for a 26-yard touchdown, and a 24-7 Detroit lead?

92. Which future Browns player ended the scoring by being on the receiving end of a 16-yard pass from third-string quarterback Jerry Reichow?

— 1964 —

93. What was the final score of the 1964 game?

94. Which Browns receiver caught three touchdown passes in the contest?

95. Who had scored an NFL record 20 touchdowns during the regular season for the Colts?

96. What weather conditions had an important effect on the outcome of the game?

97. What was the score at halftime?

98. How did Cleveland score its first points?

99. Which rookie defensive tackle played an outstanding game against the Colts' All-Star guard Jim Parker?

— 1965 —

100. How did Cleveland fare in the 1965 game?

101. Who did Green Bay have to defeat in sudden-death of their divisional playoff game to give them the right to meet the Browns?

102. Who was a hero of the game for Baltimore, stepping in to play quarterback for the first time since 1960, with the game plan taped to his wrist?

103. Bart Starr hit this end for a 47-yard touchdown pass on the first series of downs in the championship game. Name him.

104. Which two Packers each outrushed the entire Browns team in the game?

105. What was the condition of the field?

106. Which two former Browns anchored the Packer defensive line?

— 1968 —

107. Cleveland won the Century Division again in 1968, then defeated Dallas to go on to the championship game. How did they do there?

108. The tone of the game was set in Cleveland's first scoring opportunity. Who blocked Don Cockroft's 41-yard field goal attempt?

109. Whose three touchdown runs keyed the Baltimore attack?

110. Who quarterbacked the Colts in place of sore-armed Johnny Unitas?

111. What were his passing stats?

112. How many times before 1968 had the Browns been shut out?

113. Who started the scoring for the Colts?

114. How many yards did the NFL's leading rusher, Leroy Kelly, run for?

— 1969 —

115. How did the Browns do in their most recent NFL Championship Game appearance?

116. How did Cleveland fare in their regular-season meeting with Minnesota?

117. The Vikings jumped to a 14-0 lead in the first quarter. How did they get on the scoreboard?

118.   By defeating Cleveland, what first did the Vikings accomplish?

119.   What was the nickname of the Minnesota defensive front four which held the Browns in check?

Answers

1. They defeated the New York Yankees by a score of 14-9.

2. 2-0. They won by scores of 24-7 and 7-0.

3. New York's Harvey Johnson, on a 12-yard field goal in the first period

4. Marion Motley, on a one-yard plunge

5. Dante Lavelli

6. Marion Motley, with 98 yards

7. Ray Flaherty

Championship Games—Answers

8.   Spec Saunders

9.   Cleveland Stadium

10. The field was frozen and a light snow was falling.

11. The point after try was blocked, for Johnson's first miss of the season.

12. Otto Graham, at the Browns' 30 yard line.

13. Ten

14. Cleveland defeated the Yankees, by a 14-3 score.

15. Otto Graham

16. Linebacker Lou Saban

17. Horace Gillom

18. Buddy Young

19. Cleveland defeated the Buffalo Bills, 49-7.

20. Otto Graham, Marion Motley, Mac Speedie, Dante Lavelli, Lou Rymkus, Bill Willis, Ed Ulinski and Lou Saban

21. The Baltimore Colts

22. Tommy James's

23. George Ratterman

24. George Young

25. Jim Still

26. Five

27. 133 yards on 14 carries

28. Cleveland 21, San Francisco 7

29. With the League arranged in only one division, the first place team (Cleveland) and fourth place club (Buffalo) played for the right to meet the winner of the game between the second and third place teams (San Francisco, and Brooklyn-New York). In previous years, the Eastern and Western Divisional champions had met.

30. Cleveland 31, Buffalo 21; and San Francisco 17, New York 7.

31. Buck Shaw

32. Only 36, on six carries

33. Two days before the championship game

34. Lou Groza kicked a last-minute field goal to defeat the Los Angeles Rams, 30-28.

35. Rams' quarterback Bob Waterfield hit Glenn Davis with an 82-yard touchdown pass.

36. Rex Bumgardner

37. Twenty-eight seconds

38. Only nine yards on six carries

39. Joe Stydahar

40. Cleveland beat New York 8-3, and Los Angeles defeated the Chicago Bears, 24-14

41. Warren Lahr's

42. He called them the best team he had ever seen.

43. The Los Angeles Rams, by a score of 24-17

44. Lou Groza missed a 23-yard field goal.

45. Fifty-two yards

46. Dan Towler's, on a one-yard run

47. Otto Graham

48. Tom Fears

49.   Cliff Lewis and Tommy James

50.   DuMont

51. $75,000

52.   The Detroit Lions, 17-7

53.   The Los Angeles Rams, by a score of 31-21

54.   Dub Jones, Mac Speedie and John Kissell

55.   Doak Walker's

56.   None. He was injured most of the year, and only gained a total of 106 yards rushing on 26 carries.

57.   Chick Jagade, on a seven-yard run.

58.   They outgained Detroit, 384 yards to 258, and made 22 first downs to the Lions' ten

59.   Ken Carpenter

60.   Ray Renfro deflected the ball, which was caught by Pete Brewster without a defensive player making contact.

61.   Quarterback Bobby Layne

62.   Detroit again defeated the Browns, 17-16.

63. He completed only 2 of 15 passes for 20 yards. He had two tosses intercepted, fumbled once, and gained only 9 yards rushing on 5 attempts.

64. Chick Jagade

65. For the second consecutive year, Jagade scored Cleveland's only touchdown, and had identical totals of 104 yards rushing on 15 carries.

66. Jim Doran

67. Leon Hart

68. Carl Karilivacz's

69. The Detroit Lions

70. It was to be Otto Graham's final NFL game.

71. Yes, but he was coaxed into coming back during during pre-season the next year.

72. After having his first pass intercepted, leading to a Detroit field goal, Graham wound up completing 9 of 12, for 163 yards and 3 touchdowns. One pass was picked off by the Lions.

73. Chet Hanulak (44 yards)

74. Nine (six interceptions and three fumbles)

75. Frank Gatski

76. They defeated the Rams, 38-14.

77. Sid Gillman

78. Don Paul

79. He threw for 2 touchdowns and ran for 2 others, as he completed 14 of 25 passes for 209 yards.

80. Ed Modzelewski.

81. 85,693

82. He appeared in 10 championship games in his 10 years as a pro.

83. Seven

84. A 35-yard touchdown to Ray Renfro early in the fourth period.

85. They were defeated by Detroit, 59-14.

86. The San Francisco 49ers, 31-27

87. Tom Tracy, who scored two touchdowns as a replacement for the injured John Henry Johnson

88. Bobby Layne was out with a broken ankle.

89. George Wilson

90. Coach Buddy Parker walked out on the club two days before the exhibition season was to begin, after publicly denouncing the team. Assistant coach Wilson stepped in to take charge.

91. Steve Junker

92. Howard (Hopalong) Cassady

93. Cleveland shut out the favored Baltimore Colts, 27-0.

94. Gary Collins

95. Halfback Lenny Moore

96. A strong wind made passing difficult. Although the Colts' Unitas completed 12 of 20, they were good for only 95 yards.

97. 0-0

98. Kicking against the wind, Tom Gilburg of the Colts could manage only a 29-yard punt, giving Cleveland good field position. Groza then connected on a 43-yard field goal to make it 3-0 in favor of the Browns.

99. Jim Kanicki

100. They were defeated by Green Bay, 23-12.

101. The Baltimore Colts, 13-10

102. Halfback Tom Matte

103. Carroll Dale

104. Paul Hornung (105), and Jim Taylor (96) each had more yards rushing than the Browns (64).

105. The field was muddy as the result of a freezing rain.

106. Willie Davis and Henry Jordan

107. They were shut out by Baltimore, 34-0.

108. Bubba Smith

109. Tom Matte's

110. Veteran Earl Morrall

111. He completed 11 of 25, for 169 yards.

112. Only once in their history

113. Lou Michaels, with a 28-yard field goal

114.   Only 28 yards on 13 carries

115.   They bowed to Minnesota, 27-7.

116.   They were trounced by a score of 51-3.

117.   Joe Kapp rushed seven yards for the first touchdown, then hit Gene Washington on a 75-yard pass play for the second.

118.   They became the first expansion team to win an NFL title.

119.   "The Purple People Eaters"

Records and Honors

1. Which Browns player was the first football player to win the coveted Hickok Belt as "Professional Athlete of the Year"?

2. In what year did he win the award?

3. Jim Brown's 126 career touchdowns shattered the former league record of 105. Who held the previous mark?

4. How many times did Brown lead the NFL in rushing?

5. Which former Browns player was inducted into the Pro Football Hall of Fame in 1982?

6. Lou Groza's streak of consecutive PATs was broken in 1953. How many kicks in succession did he make?

7. The Browns' 42-21 win over Chicago in 1951 was memorable for what reason?

8. Whose play highlighted the game?

9. Who was named the Outstanding Back in the 1962 and 1966 NFL Pro Bowl games, and Player of the Game in the 1963 contest?

10. Who holds the Browns' NFL record for most touchdown receptions in a career?

11. Who did Otto Graham combine with on a 99-yard touchdown play in 1947?

12. Name the Cleveland linebacker named by The Associated Press as the NFL Defensive Rookie of the Year in 1983.

13. Who did A.P. name as the NFL's Most Valuable Player in 1981?

14. Who holds the record for playing the most seasons with the Browns?

15. Who won the Hickok Belt in 1964?

16. In how many consecutive games did Lou Groza score between 1950 and 1953?

17. Which Browns great was elected to the Hall of Fame in 1976?

18. Who won the first Browns' Most Valuable Player award from the Cleveland Touchdown Club (1954)?

19. Which Browns player kicked a 60-yard field goal in a 1984 game, setting a Cleveland record?

20. Who did he kick it against?

21. Who caught a club-record 89 passes in 1983, then repeated the feat the next season?

22. Which Browns kicker led the NFL in punting in 1965?

23. In 1985, Cleveland had two backs who each gained over 1,000 yards rushing, becoming only the third team in NFL history ever to have such a tandem. Can you name the players?

24. Which former Browns player was inducted into the Hall of Fame in 1984?

25. Who was the Player of the Game in the first Pro Bowl game, back in 1951?

26. Which other Browns were Pro Bowl representatives that season?

27. Can you name the first five Browns rookies to garner Pro Bowl honors?

28. Which Browns player was named Player of the Game in the 1957 Pro Bowl?

29. In which three consecutive seasons did Mike Pruitt gain 1,000 or more yards rushing?

30. Which player had 12 quarterback sacks in 1984, setting a club record for linebackers?

31. In 1985, he became the first Browns player in 18 years to return a punt for a touchdown, streaking 37 yards against the New York Jets. Can you name this player?

32. Which Brown made Pro Bowl appearances while with Chicago and New York, as well as with Cleveland?

33. Who holds the Cleveland record for most kickoff and punt returns?

34. Which two future Browns were co-MVPs in the 1958 game when the Chicago College All-Stars upset the Detroit Lions, 35-19?

35. Who is the only Browns' season punting leader not to total at least 1,000 yards with his kicks?

36. In a 1951 game, the Browns and Bears were assessed a total of 374 yards in penalties. That was more than the Browns accumulated in all of 1959. How many yards were they penalized that year?

37. Who was Cleveland's opponent when Jim Brown scored his 106th NFL touchdown to set a league record?

38. What other milestone was surpassed in that same game?

39. Which Cleveland quarterback was the NFL's passing leader for two successive years?

40. Who holds the Cleveland record for rushing yards in a playoff game?

41. Who are the only non-kickers to lead Cleveland in scoring since 1950?

42. Who led Cleveland in rushing in 1973, although he had no run from scrimmage longer than 17 yards?

43. Who had a club-leading 63 receptions in 1980, but not a single touchdown catch?

44. Which Browns player appeared in the most consecutive games?

45. How many of these were consecutive starts?

46. Which former Browns player was elected to the Hall of Fame in 1983?

47. Since 1950, which three Browns have returned two interceptions for touchdowns in a single season?

48. Name the player who averaged nearly 30 yards per kickoff return for Cleveland in 1954?

49. Which three players have scored four touchdowns in a game against Cleveland?

50. Jim Brown set Pro Bowl rushing records in two successive seasons (1962 and 1963). How many yards did he gain in each game?

51. Who is the only non-quarterback to fumble four times in a game for the Browns since 1950?

52. Which two Browns had highly uncharacteristic performances in the 1955 Pro Bowl game?

53. Which team blocked a Lou Groza PAT try, breaking his streak of 121 successful kicks (109 in the NFL)?

54. Who was Cleveland's opponent in the game in which Jim Brown passed Joe Perry as the NFL's all-time leading rusher?

55. Which rookie returned a kickoff 102 yards for a touchdown in a 1958 game against the Chicago Cardinals?

56. Which Cleveland record-setting play highlighted the Browns' 27-20 victory over Denver on "Floyd Little Day," October 29, 1972?

57. Who were the victims of Jim Brown's first 100-yard rushing game of his career?

58. Who was Cleveland's opponent in 1963 when Jim Brown passed Ollie Matson as the NFL's all-time leader in total yards?

59. Who is the only Browns player since 1950 to have totaled more than 300 yards in punt returns in a single season?

60. Who returned two punts for touchdowns in 1965?

61. Can you name the Browns' record-holder (since 1950) for the longest kickoff return?

62. Who did Lou Groza surpass when he became the NFL's all-time leading scorer in 1961?

63. Which former Browns player was inducted into the Hall of Fame in 1985?

64. How many field goals did Don Cockroft attempt in the October 19, 1975 game against Denver?

65. Of those, how many did he connect on?

66. How many consecutive 100-yard rushing games did Jim Brown have in 1958?

67. How many times in his career did Jim Brown gain 100 yards rushing in a game?

68. How many times have Brown players rushed for 1,000 yards in a season?

69. Gerald McNeil set a Cleveland NFL record for longest punt return, in a 1986 game against Dallas. How long was it?

70. Jim Brown set a major college scoring record in a 1956 game against Colgate. How many points did he score that day?

71. How many consecutive field goals did Don Cockroft make in a streak which extended from 1974 to 1975?

72. When Otto Graham was elected to the Hall of Fame in 1965, he became the youngest ever inducted. How old was he?

73. Whose overtime field goal in the Browns' 13-10 win over Houston in 1986 gave him an NFL record five overtime kicks?

74. Which former Browns player once fumbled seven times in a game while with Kansas City?

75. Bernie Kosar finished the 1986 regular season with the best interception ratio in the league. How many of his passes were picked off?

76. Who had 32 receptions to lead the 1974 squad, but not a single one for a touchdown?

77. Who is the only Browns player to have kicked 300 field goals in his NFL career? Hint: most of them were made with another team.

78. Who is the only Cleveland player since 1950 to have totaled more than 1,000 yards on kickoff returns in a season?

79. Whose record for career catches by a tight end did Ozzie Newsome break?

80. Which Browns player was voted the Miller Lite Offensive Lineman of the Year for 1986?

Answers

1.   Otto Graham

2.   1956

3.   Don Hutson

4.   Seven (1957, 1958, 1960, 1961, 1963, 1964 and 1965)

5.   Doug Atkins

6.   109

7.   They were assessed an NFL record 209 yards in penalties.

Records and Honors—Answers

8.   Dub Jones's. He scored six touchdowns to tie the NFL mark set by Ernie Nevers in 1929.

9.   Jim Brown

10. Gary Collins (70)

11. Mac Speedie

12. Chip Banks

13. Brian Sipe

14. Lou Groza (21)

15. Jim Brown

16. 45

17. Len Ford

18. Len Ford

19. Steve Cox

20. The Cincinnati Bengals (October 21, 1984)

21. Ozzie Newsome

22. Gary Collins

23. Kevin Mack and Earnest Byner

24. Mike McCormack

25. Otto Graham

26. Tony Adamle, Lou Groza, Weldon Humble, Marion Motley, Mac Speedie and Bill Willis

27. Jim Brown (1957), Paul Warfield (1964), Greg Pruitt (1973), Chip Banks (1982) and Kevin Mack (1985)

28. Otto Graham

29. 1979, 1980 and 1981

30. Clay Matthews

31. Brian Brennan

32. Erich Barnes

33. Dino Hall (151 kickoff returns and 111 punt returns)

34. Bobby Mitchell and Jim Ninowski

35. Junior Wren, who had 996 yards on 27 punts in 1959

36. 329

37. The Philadelphia Eagles (October 3, 1965)

38. Lou Groza appeared in his 177th NFL game, topping Y. A. Tittle's previous high of 176.

39. Milt Plum (1960 and 1961)

40. Earnest Byner (161 versus Miami on January 4, 1986)

41. Jim Brown (five times), and Leroy Kelly (three times)

42. Ken Brown

43. Mike Pruitt

44. Doug Dieken (203)

45. 194

46. Paul Warfield

47. Warren Lahr (1951), Ken Konz (1954) and Bobby Franklin (1960)

48. Billy Reynolds (29.5)

49. Pittsburgh's Ray Mathews (October 17, 1954), Green Bay's Jim Taylor (October 15, 1961) and Green Bay's Donny Anderson (November 12, 1967)

50. 120 yards in 1962, and 141 the next year

51.   Running back Ken Brown (October 8, 1972, versus Kansas City)

52.   Otto Graham, who completed only 4 of 17 passes, and Lou Groza, who missed two of three PATs

53.   The Chicago Cardinals (October 4, 1953)

54.   The Philadelphia Eagles (October 20, 1963)

55.   Leroy Bolden

56.   Don Cockroft's 57-yard field goal

57.   The Washington Redskins (November 3, 1957)

58.   The St. Louis Cardinals (November 17, 1963)

59.   Greg Pruitt (349 in 1974)

60.   Leroy Kelly

61.   Carl Ward (104 yards, on November 5, 1967)

62.   Don Hutson

63.   Frank Gatski

64.   Seven

Records and Honors—Answers

65. Five

66. Six

67. 58 times

68. As of 1987, six Browns have reached the 1,000-yard mark a total of 19 times.

69. 84 yards

70. 43

71. 16 (11 in 1974 and five in 1975)

72. 43

73. Mark Moseley's. He had been signed less than a week earlier.

74. Len Dawson

75. Only 10 of 531

76. Hugh McKinnis

77. Mark Moseley

78. Dino Hall (1,014 in 1979)

79. Jackie Smith's

80. Center Mike Baab

Miscellaneous

1. This former Browns player once returned an interception 102 yards for a touchdown while with the Giants (October 22, 1961). Can you name him?

2. Which former Heisman Trophy winner played for Cleveland in 1962?

3. What was kicker Sam Baker's given name?

4. Which Browns Hall-of-Famer grew up in Canton, Ohio, the site of the football shrine?

5. How many college games did Dante Lavelli play in ?

6. Which Cleveland all-pro was also a basketball All-America at Northwestern?

7. Which Browns running star was picked in the eighth round of the 1958 draft?

8. Who was the quarterback that Cleveland obtained in a 1960 deal with the Steelers?

9. Lou Groza's uniform was retired when he decided to hang up his cleats for good before the 1968 season. What was his number?

10. Can you name the quarterback the Browns obtained from Pittsburgh in a 1968 trade?

11. What future NFL general manager did the Browns take in the third round of the 1952 draft?

12. Name the Browns' defensive back who was electrocuted in a construction accident in June of 1963.

13. Cleveland Stadium is the nation's largest facility to be home to both a major league baseball team and an NFL club. What is its seating capacity?

14. Which former NBA player is the vice president of Operations at Cleveland Stadium?

15. Which future NFL coach did the Browns choose in the ninth round of the 1951 draft?

16. Who did Cleveland receive from the Giants in the 1970 trade that sent Ron Johnson, Wayne Meylan and Jim Kanicki to New York?

17. Which Cleveland pick in the 1973 draft was runner-up in the 1972 Heisman Trophy voting?

18. Which Browns defensive back played minor league baseball in 1958?

19. In whose farm system did he play?

20. Which future Green Bay all-pro was chosen in the fifth round in 1957, with a pick acquired from the Packers?

21. Who was the 1956 Olympic gold medal winner who spent 1957 with the Browns?

22. In which event was he victorious?

23. Can you name the major league baseball team which offered Jim Brown a contract in 1959?

24. Who was selected as the NFL's first President?

25. When was he elected?

26. Who was the first Cleveland player to jump to the new United States Football League in 1983?

27. After missing the 1954 season due to injuries, Marion Motley attempted a comeback in 1955 at what position?

28. After Ernie Davis died of leukemia in 1963, Cleveland retired his uniform. What was his number?

29. Which top draft pick turned down a $900,000 four-year contract with Cleveland in 1983 for a shot at the 1984 Olympics?

30. Which 1981 draft choice was the nation's leading punter in 1980?

31. Name the CFL and AFL star who had a tryout with the Browns in 1954 as an 18-year old running back.

32. Who was the former NFL star hired by Cleveland in 1982 as a special consultant?

33. Which future NFL coach was traded to Green Bay in 1951 in exchange for Dan Orlich?

34. In 1983, this Browns player underwent successful brain surgery for internal hydrocephalus. Can you name him?

35. Who did the Browns receive from Pittsburgh in exchange for Marion Motley and a draft choice in a 1955 deal?

36. Who was the Browns' second draft pick in 1957, after Jim Brown?

37. Which Ohio State basketball star was Cleveland's seventh-round draft choice in 1962?

38. Which Cleveland player jumped to the New Jersey Generals of the USFL in December of 1983?

39. Which future Hall-of-Famer did the Browns send to the New York Yankees, together with Sisto Averno, for a 1952 draft pick who turned out to be quarterback Don Klosterman?

40. Name the veteran end of the Browns picked by Dallas in the 1960 expansion draft.

41. Who was involved in the trade of centers between Cleveland and Los Angeles in 1960?

42. Who was the first black player to win the Heisman Trophy?

43. Which future Buffalo Bills star was signed by Cleveland in 1959, but released without playing in a single game?

44. Which Browns running back was the first black to play at Oklahoma?

45. What position was the highest that Jim Brown placed in the Heisman Trophy voting?

46. Who finished ahead of him?

47. Which former Browns' star preceded Vince Lombardi as head coach of the Washington Redskins?

48. Who did Cleveland receive from Dallas when they sent all-pro guard Jim Ray Smith to the Cowboys in 1963?

49. Why was a special rule needed to allow Bernie Kosar to play in the NFL?

50. Who did the Browns send to the New York Giants in 1964 in exchange for Dick Modzelewski?

51. Which team claimed Leroy Kelly on waivers in 1974?

52. Who did Cleveland send to New England in exchange for wide receiver Reggie Rucker?

53. Name the Browns player who was born four days after Cleveland played its first NFL game (September 16, 1950).

54. Which Browns player has a brother who played on the 1972 U.S. Olympic soccer team?

55. Which Browns linebacker is the son of a Hall of Fame linebacker?

56. The fathers of which two Browns' teammates were roommates at Indiana University for one year? Hint: One of the players is an ex-Brown.

57. Which Cleveland kicker spent two years in the New York Mets' farm system as a third baseman?

58. What Boston University great did Cleveland draft in the first round in 1952?

59. Which Browns player has a brother who played for the Cleveland Indians?

60. The Browns are the only NFL club whose helmets do not include what?

61. How did Otto Graham perform in his final collegiate game?

62. Which other future Browns also played for the Chicago All-Stars in that game?

63. Who is the former Browns' Director of Player Personnel who was the son of a former major league baseball player and manager?

64. Which Browns player performed in all 10 seasons of the AFL's existence?

65. What was his given name?

66. Who was Cleveland's first draft pick in their initial NFL season?

67. What college was he from?

68. Which Browns star played professional basketball with the Rochester Royals of the NBL in the 1945-1946 season?

69. How many games did he play in and how many points per game did he average?

70. Name two NFL officials who formerly played with the Browns.

71. Who is the NFL lineman who married the daughter of Hall-of-Famer Jim Brown?

72. What team did Paul Warfield play for in the WFL?

73. Which former Browns player has a brother who was an American League batting champion?

74. Who coached the Chicago College All-Stars the greatest number of times?

75. How many times?

76. Which Cowboys defensive end became involved in a fight with Jim Brown which nearly precipitated a riot in a 1964 game?

77. Although he never played with Cleveland, this eighth-round future pick in 1961 went on to score in an NFL record 151 straight games, and later invented the Nerf ball. Can you name him?

78. Which Brown's father played for Cleveland back in 1951?

79. Which Browns owner was responsible for introducing the term "taxi squad" into football vernacular?

80. Purdue's MVP in 1962, this Cleveland sixth-round choice was killed in an auto

accident in January of 1963. Do you remember him?

81. Which former Browns kicker tied Lou Groza's single-game record of eight PATs, while with Detroit in 1957?

82. Which NFL club has never beaten the Browns in regular-season play?

83. Which team has Cleveland defeated only once in its history?

84. Which member of the Cleveland organization is married to TV and movie actress Patricia Breslin?

85. How did Jim Brown score his first NFL touchdown?

86. Which future NFL coach was drafted by Cleveland in the 20th round in 1953?

87. Which two Browns served as pit-crew members for Indianapolis 500 driver Scott Brayton?

88. Who was the last of the "original" Browns to retire?

89. Who is the only player to gain 200 yards rushing in a game against Cleveland?

90. Which Cincinnati back had an 86-yard touchdown run against the Browns in 1971 for the longest-ever run from scrimmage against Cleveland?

91. Which former Brown kicked a then-NFL record 56-yard field goal in his first attempt in a league game?

92. Which former Columbia University quarterback spent two years on the Browns' taxi squad after being picked in the first round of the 1965 draft, but never appeared in a regular season game?

93. Which Browns player's Ph.D. dissertation was entitled, "A Characterization of the Set of Asymptotic Values of a Function Homomorphic in the Unit Disc"?

94. Which former Brown was a student of the Chinese language Mandarin?

95. Which Giants tight end was originally a 17th-round pick of the Browns in 1953, but never played for them?

96. Which former Browns player became coach of the first team to play in three straight Super Bowls?

97. Who did Cleveland draft with the first-round pick obtained from Miami in exchange for Paul Warfield?

98. Who suffered a broken ankle while playing in a benefit game for the Browns' basketball team in 1983?

99. Who did Cleveland send to Washington in exchange for Sam Baker in 1960?

100. Whom did Art Modell call, "The finest boy I have ever met in my life"?

101. What was noteworthy about the Browns-Falcons exhibition game in 1973?

102. Which two Browns players were among the seven players ejected for fighting in Cleveland's 24-7 victory over Philadelphia on October 13, 1957?

103. In a 1959 game against Cleveland, both Chicago Cardinal quarterbacks, King Hill and M. C. Reynolds, were knocked out of action. Who was the defensive back who took over and threw a 62-yard touchdown pass against the surprised Browns?

104. Which future Hall-of-Famer was sent to Green Bay in exchange for A.D. Williams in 1960?

105. Where was the first NFL Players Association formed?

106. Which Washington lineman died of coronary thrombosis following the Redskins-Browns game in 1954?

107. Which Browns player had a brother who was an All-America basketball player at Kentucky and later a star in the NBA?

108. Which Philadelphia Eagles player returned a missed field goal attempt 100 yards for a touchdown, sparking a 33-21 upset of the Browns in 1966?

109. Which Browns player played professional basketball with the Dayton Rens?

110. What unusual play gave Cleveland its first score in Dick Modzelewski's game as interim coach in 1977?

111. Which two kickers were traded by Cleveland in 1966, and went on to have successful careers with their new clubs?

112. Which brothers played for Cleveland, and had another brother who played elsewhere in the NFL?

113. Which future NFL star was sent to San Francisco in a 1968 deal for a second-round draft pick?

114. Which star receiver did Cleveland obtain from Green Bay in 1950, then turn

around and send to San Francisco 12 days later?

115. Who did Buffalo select with the number-one draft pick they obtained from Cleveland in the Tom Cousineau deal?

116. Knowing that Otto Graham would return in 1955 if needed, Paul Brown turned down this young quarterback in his quest for a shot at the Browns. Who was this future NFL great?

117. Many of the records set by Jim Brown at Syracuse University were later broken by which Heisman Trophy winner?

118. Which NFL club has Cleveland played, beaten, and lost to more than any other team?

119. Since 1978, the Browns have picked a player from a California school with their top draft choice every even year. Can you name these five California collegians?

120. How did Bernie Parrish spark a controversy in 1965?

121. Which two Browns were "presenters" for each other when they were inducted into the Hall of Fame?

122. A broken jaw suffered by Otto Graham in 1955 gave way to what NFL innovation?

123. Which Browns running back worked as a stand-in for Burt Reynolds in the movie "Semi-Tough"?

124. Which Browns wide receiver has a son who was also a wide receiver in the NFL?

125. Who did Bernie Kosar start ahead of while leading Miami to the 1983 National Championship?

126. Some Browns play "Cooz Ball" as a training exercise. "Cooz Ball" is played with perforated paddles and a Whiffle ball, on half a tennis court. Who invented it?

127. Who was the lightest player in the NFL in 1986?

128. How much did he weigh?

129. In one of their worst trades, the Browns sent Jim Marshall, Paul Dickson, Jamie Caleb, Jim Prestel, Dick Grecni and Bill Gault to Minnesota in exchange for two picks in the 1962 draft. Who were the two players chosen by Cleveland, neither of whom ever made it into a regular-season game with the Browns?

130. Prior to beating them in 1986, how many consecutive times had the Browns lost to the Steelers in Pittsburgh?

131. In 1957, this kicker tied Lou Groza for the NFL scoring lead. In 1960, he was traded to Cleveland. Who was he?

132. How many "Browns" have played for Cleveland?

133. Can you name them?

134. Which kicker, drafted in the second round in 1977, refused to sign with Cleveland and was eventually dealt to Detroit where he became one of the NFL's top punters?

135. How many overtime games did the Browns play in 1986?

136. Only three Cleveland Browns have had the initials C.B. How many can you name?

Answers

1.   Erich Barnes

2.   Howard (Hopalong) Cassady

3.   Loris

4.   Marion Motley

5.   Only three varsity games at Ohio State

6.   Otto Graham

7.   Bobby Mitchell

8.   Len Dawson

Miscellaneous—Answers

9.   76

10.   Bill Nelsen

11.   Don Klosterman

12.   Don Fleming

13.   80,098

14.   Larry Staverman

15.   Don Shula

16.   Homer Jones

17.   Greg Pruitt

18.   Bernie Parrish

19.   The Cincinnati Reds

20.   Henry Jordan

21.   Milt Campbell

22.   The decathlon

23.   The Cleveland Indians

24.   Art Modell

25.   1967

26. Running back Cleo Miller

27. Linebacker

28. 45

29. Ron Brown

30. Steve Cox

31. Cookie Gilchrist

32. Calvin Hill

33. Walt Michaels

34. Steve Cox

35. Ed Modzelewski

36. Quarterback Milt Plum

37. John Havlicek

38. Quarterback Brian Sipe

39. Art Donovan

40. Billy Howton

41. Art Hunter, who went to the Rams, and John Morrow

42. Syracuse's Ernie Davis (1961)

43. Elbert Dubenion

44. Prentice Gautt

45. Fifth (1956)

46. Paul Hornung, Johnny Majors, Tommy McDonald and Jerry Tubbs

47. Otto Graham (1966-1968)

48. Tackle Monte Clark

49. He graduated from the University of Miami a year ahead of his class.

50. End Bobby Crespino

51. The Oakland Raiders. He did not make the squad, however.

52. A fourth-round draft pick, who turned out to be Allen Carter

53. Defensive end Ernie Price (September 20, 1950)

54. Matt Bahr (brother Casey)

55. Bobby Bell (father Bobby, Sr. of the Kansas Chiefs)

56.   Bob Golic and Tom Cousineau

57.   Punter Jeff Gossett

58.   Harry Agganis

59.   Mike Pagel (brother Karl)

60.   A team logo

61.   He led the Chicago College All-Stars to a 16-0 victory over the NFL champion Los Angeles Rams on August 24, 1946.

62.   Dub Jones, Darrell Palmer, Lou Saban and John Yonakor

63.   Tommy Prothro, son of "Doc" Prothro

64.   Babe Parilli

65.   Vito

66.   Ken Carpenter

67.   Oregon State

68.   Otto Graham

69.   He appeared in 32 games and averaged 5.2 points per game.

70. Pete Liske and Gary Lane

71. Chris Ward

72. The Memphis Southmen, also known as the Grizzlies

73. Ron Johnson (brother Alex)

74. Otto Graham

75. Ten

76. George Andrie

77. Fred Cox

78. Jack Gregory

79. Mickey McBride. He used to have fringe players drive for his taxicab company until their services were needed.

80. Defensive back Tom Bloom

81. Jim Martin

82. Tampa Bay

83. Los Angeles Raiders

84. Owner Art Modell

85. Brown caught a five-yard pass from quarterback Tom O'Connell against the Philadelphia Eagles in his third pro game (October 13, 1957).

86. Chuck Noll

87. Bob Golic and Tom Cousineau

88. Lou Groza

89. John Henry Johnson (with exactly 200 on October 10, 1964)

90. Essex Johnson

91. Bert Rechichar, then with Baltimore, against the Chicago Bears on September 27, 1953

92. Archie Roberts

93. Frank Ryan

94. Lou Saban

95. Bob Schnelker

96. Don Shula

97. Quarterback Mike Phipps

98. Dave Logan

99. Bob Khayat and Fran O'Brien

100. Ernie Davis

101. It was the first pro game ever played at the University of Tennessee.

102. Bill Quinlan and Paul Wiggins

103. John Roach

104. Willie Davis

105. In the basement of Dante Lavelli's home in Cleveland

106. Dave Sparks

107. Lou Groza (brother Alex)

108. Al Nelson

109. Len Ford

110. Quarterback Terry Luck let the snap go through his legs to running back Greg Pruitt. Pruitt then passed to a diving Luck in the end zone for the score.

111. Punter David Lee (Baltimore) and placekicker David Ray (Los Angeles)

112. Jim and Lin Houston (brother Walt)

113. Clifton McNeil

114. Gordy Soltau

115. Quarterback Jim Kelly

116. Johnny Unitas

117. Ernie Davis

118. The Pittsburgh Steelers (43-31 in 74 games)

119. Clay Matthews (USC in 1978), Charles White (USC in 1980), Chip Banks (USC in 1982), Don Rogers (UCLA in 1984), and Webster Slaughter (San Diego State in 1986)

120. He said that former coach Paul Brown should replace Pete Rozelle as Commissioner of the NFL.

121. Otto Graham and Paul Brown

122. Single bar protectors on helmets

123. Brian Duncan

124. Ray Renfro (son Mike)

125. Vinny Testaverde

126. Tom Cousineau

127. Gerald McNeil

128. 143 pounds

129. Defensive tackle Charles Hinton and end Ronnie Myers

130. 16

131. Sam Baker

132. Nine

133. Wide receiver Stan Brown (1971), defensive back Dean Brown (1969), running back Jim Brown (1957-1965), tackle John Brown (1962-66), running back Ken Brown (1970-1975), defensive back Eddie Brown (1974-1975), defensive back Terry Brown (1976), defensive end Tom Brown (1981) and kick returner Preston Brown (1984)

134. Tom Skladany

135. Four (two in regular-season games, and two in postseason competition)

136. Carl Barisich, Clifford Brooks and Clinton Burrell (Chip Banks' given first name is William)

Photos

1. This coach once noted, "A winner never whines." Identify him.

NFL Photos

2. In 1972 this Hall-of-Famer died at the young age of forty-six. Name him.

NFL Photos

3. A standout in college, this running back caught an 87-yard pass in the 1960 Cotton Bowl for a major-bowl-game record. Who was he?

NFL Photos

4. Maryland coach Tom Nugent said of this All-American: "He's in a class all by himself." To whom was he referring?

NFL Photos

5. Name this former Brown, who was a star with Chicago's Monsters of the Midway for twelve seasons before finishing his career with the New Orleans Saints.

NFL Photos

6. This former Brown became the first black to play for the Washington Redskins. Name him.

NFL Photos

7. Name this man, who holds the NFL mark for highest pass rating for a single season with 110.4 in 1960.

NFL Photos

8. This running back was once named by *Esquire* magazine as one of the best-dressed athletes in America. Identify him.

NFL Photos

9. Name this former Cleveland linebacker who was traded to San Diego on April 28, the day of the 1987 college draft.

The Cleveland Browns

10. Name this Cleveland star who once said, "Old placekickers never die, they just go on missing the point."

The Cleveland Browns

11. In the first game of the 1987 season, Ozzie Newsome moved into tenth place on the all-time NFL list for career receptions. Who did he surpass to move into this spot?

The Cleveland Browns

12. Identify this running back, who led Cleveland in both rushing and scoring in 1986 despite playing in only twelve games due to injury.

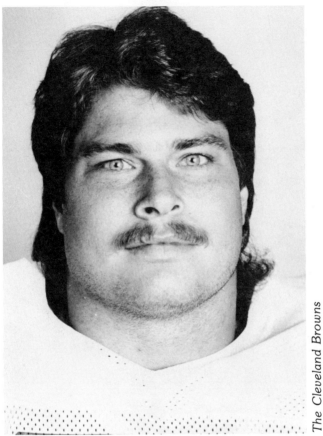

The Cleveland Browns

13. Name this offensive lineman who attended Tarrant County Junior College, Austin Community College and the University of Texas?

The Cleveland Browns

14. Name this USC linebacker, who was a first-round pick of the Browns in the 1978 draft.

The Cleveland Browns

15.   Only one Brown was named AFC offen-
        sive player of the week in 1986. Can you
        name him?

NFL Photos

16. How many times did Jim Brown lead the NFL in touchdowns?

The Cleveland Browns

17.　This quarterback passed to Dave Logan to set up the winning field goal in the Browns' first overtime game ever, on September 26, 1977. Name him.

The Cleveland Browns

18. Name this receiver, whose nickname was "Rhino."

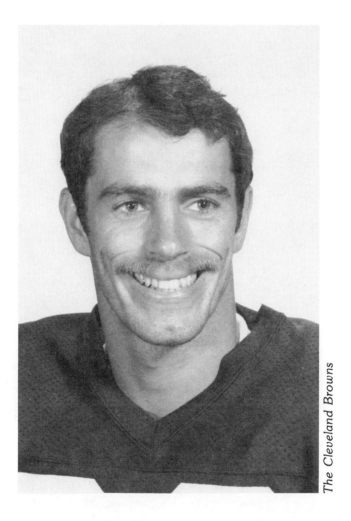

The Cleveland Browns

19.　　In 1979 this Browns rookie returned fifty kickoffs. Who is he?

The Cleveland Browns

20.   This end received bonus offers from several major league baseball clubs before deciding on a career in pro football. Name him.

The Cleveland Browns

21. Can you name this all-time Cleveland great who recovered four of his own fumbles in a 1953 game against the Giants to set an NFL mark?

The Cleveland Browns

22. Where did star center Frank Gatski attend college?

The Cleveland Browns

23.   This end intended going to Notre Dame but changed his mind and went to Ohio State when the Buckeyes hired Paul Brown as their coach in 1941. Who was this star who was reunited with his college mentor in the pros?

The Cleveland Browns

24. This all-time great played for McKinley High School. In his three years they lost only three games, each one to Massillon, coached by Paul Brown. Name this running back, who later played for Brown at Cleveland.

The Cleveland Browns

25. Name this Browns running back, who was a cousin of former NBA star Bob Love.

The Cleveland Browns

26. In Cleveland's first NFL season of 1950, Mac Speedie led all their receivers with 42 catches. How many were for touchdowns?

The Cleveland Browns

27. When was the construction of Cleveland Stadium completed?

Answers

1. Paul Brown

2. Len Ford

3. Ernie Davis

4. Gary Collins

5 Doug Atkins

6. Bobby Mitchell

7. Milt Plum

8. Leroy Kelly

9.   Chip Banks

10. Lou Groza

11. Lance Alworth

12. Kevin Mack

13. Mike Baab

14. Clay Matthews

15. Bernie Kosar

16. Five times: 1957 through 1959, 1963 and 1965

17. Brian Sipe

18. Homer Jones

19. Dino Hall

20. Paul Warfield

21. Otto Graham

22. Marshall University

23. Dante Lavelli

24. Marion Motley

Photos—Answers

25. Greg Pruitt

26. Only one

27. July, 1931